Feather Press Publishing
Second edition published in March 2021
kerrie@theinteriorco.co.uk
Info@theinteriorco.co.uk

Written and produced by Kerrie Griffin

FROM SHED TO CHIC

Shed to Chic is about one woman's dream to turn her garage into a money-making holiday cottage. It shows that all it takes is drive and motivation and that, by making the right choices with simple touches and the right attention to detail, you too can be inspired to create a perfect space for luxury holiday lets.

This is your go-to guide on how to create a money-making holiday let.
I wanted to create an experience like a hotel in a holiday let.

It can be a real money-spinner to pay off your mortgage early. This guide shows you how to make an income from your home. You could be earning in the region of £32,000 per year by converting your garage into a luxury holiday let and be fully booked for six months within a short period of opening if you follow my guide.

I believe I've got the recipe right. If you follow my guide, I am sure you will create something extraordinary for people to visit, create memories, and write about in beautiful interior magazines.

DREAM – VISION – CREATE – REALITY

FROM SHED TO CHIC

Not only is it a helpful guide offering practical advice and top tips on anything from building regulations and planning to which holiday let company to choose, but it is also a story of endurance and determination which will inspire others.

I am a well-established interior designer and artist who founded the Interior Co in 1997 to offer interior lifestyle and products under one roof. In turn, I worked my magic on "Turtledove Hideaway," when, with an investment of £10,000, I created a sought-after retreat for couples which was listed with the selective Unique Homestays for three years until it was established in its own right.

My unique retreat, Turtledove Hideaway, has appeared on the front cover of an Italian magazine and has been featured in Germany and Canada, featured in the Sunday Telegraph, The Times, and The Daily Mail, along with House Beautiful magazine.

DREAM – VISION – CREATE – REALITY

FROM SHED TO CHIC

My work as an interior designer has been featured in many magazines, including Country Homes & Interiors, 25 Beautiful Homes, Ideal Home, and the high-profile Italian magazine, Ristrutturare.

I am considered a successful artist, and two of my famous feather design paintings have sold to American clients as a direct result of appearing in international interior magazines. The Times, The Telegraph and The Daily Mail have applauded me for my "fantastic creativity" along with interior designers and architects from around the globe.

There's nothing quite like reading the guest book after they have left – it's the first thing I can't wait to do!

Kerrie Griffin
Multi-Award-Winning Interior Designer

DREAM – VISION – CREATE – REALITY

DEDICATION

I want to dedicate this book to my friends for the love and support you showed me when I was pulling my hair out with creativity racing through my body, yet not a penny to my name to be able to act on it.

Richard, you encouraged and helped me; thank you. To my daughters for making me want to live another day to create a better future for them and show them that mummy has got this! Jasmin and Hannah, I love you. You see, I had a dream to turn my garage into a cottage when most said "it can't be done," but I'm afraid Sagittarians don't know the meaning of "can't"; they are doers they go to the end of the earth to make sure it happens. Add one Sagittarius woman to an "it's not possible" and, hey presto, it's like magic; she makes it happen regardless of obstacles.

I scrimped and saved and sold everything I didn't use to get enough money to start to turn my dream into reality, and it has totally paid off as this little garage now pays my mortgage.

If you are thinking, "Ah, that would be nice," and you are talkers and dreamers who never take the plunge, take it from me; dream a little and get on and do it. Your dream could be to pay your mortgage in no time.
Kerrie

DREAM – VISION – CREATE – REALITY

A DREAM BECOMES REALITY

Finnnished!

I used to tie the ponies up to be shod inside where the kitchen is now

DREAM – VISION – CREATE – REALITY

The Telegraph – October 2013 – This Is Money photo and article.
Ristrutturare Con Casa Chic – October 2013
Home Bunch (Canada) – May 2013
Westwing Magazine (Germany) – June 2013
House Beautiful – September 2013
The Sunday Times (online) – October 2013
Wedding magazine – November 2013
Evening Standard – Homes & Properties November 2013
Reader Sheds Entry Reader Sheds Andrew Wilcox From Grand Designs and Small spaces competition.
http://www.readersheds.co.uk/share.cfm?SHARESHED=4847English
Home Magazine – Small Spaces

Casa da Sogno (Italian magazine) – January 2014
Home Builders and Renovators – May 2014
Ideal Home – July 2014

Yorkshire Living – December 2016

Listed as one of ten of the most amazing tiny cottages in the UK – February 2015

The Sunday Times
WalesOnline   -
https://www.walesonline.co.uk/lifestyle/welsh-homes/rural-welsh-dream-home-could-14869849

UNUSUAL PIECES - INTERESTING FINDS - UNIQUE PROPERTY

Courage award – Nov 2019 Positivity Awards Amanda Moss, Awarded for courage in adversity.

Winner of Highly Commended – Residential Interior Designer of the Year – NDA – Nov 2017

"I am thrilled to have been awarded Highly Commended for this year's Northern Design Awards. The judges took an extra week to deliberate this category of Residential Interior Designer of the Year."

"This year's entries were substantial," said Shelly Bond, Director of Events at Jazz Productions, who organises these prestigious awards for the north of the country.

"Last Year, my work was chosen by **Linda Barker** and **Paul Smith** and I was awarded a **Finalist**. It was amongst hundreds of strong entries. I attended the star-studded event in Leeds, where I was one of four others in her category of **Residential Interior Designer of the Year.** We didn't win, but our work has been recognised on the big screen, and the cheer for the design shown on the night was immense; we made lots of contacts and hope by winning this, and this year now achieving Commended, people will recognise we mean business. I have a real passion for older properties, and I intend to keep trying to get them noticed, and maybe next year I aim to win."

UNUSUAL PIECES – INTERESTING FINDS – UNIQUE PROPERTY

Nominated for Womenspire Awards May 2017
"Congratulations: You are truly inspirational!"
You have been nominated for Chwarae Teg's Womenspire 2017 Awards."

"You should be proud that your achievements are genuinely valued, recognised, and are being seen as making a big difference to women in Wales."

PROFESSIONALS - MEDIA COVERAGE - LUXURY RENTAL MARKET

Finalist – Best Country Home of the Year – Period Living Magazine Nov 2016

Nov 2016 Period Living Magazine WINNER
"Kerrie Griffin and her company, The Interior Co, created a fantastic country home and she was awarded Best Country Home."

Finalist Residential Interior Designer of the Year – Northern Design Awards
Oct 2016.

CONGRATULATIONS – MEDIA COVERAGE – LUXURY RENTAL MARKET

Residential Interior Designer of the Year

"We very much look forward to welcoming you to the celebrations at the iconic Royal Armouries Museum on Friday 11 November. A night of fantastic entertainment, great food, and networking await, where we shall be announcing the winners in a glittering night with all of our 2016 judges, finalists, and special guests."

WINNER Best Country Home of the Year (Period Living Magazine) Aug 2016

"The Interior Co's office is an oak-framed period property in the Welsh/Shropshire hills. She transformed it and is now up for an award already placed as one of five in the country. They await the winner's decision. Step inside The Interior Co's period property, which was the start of her online shopping revolution, and see how she transformed it into an award-winning home."

CONGRATULATIONS - MEDIA COVERAGE - LUXURY RENTAL MARKET

My Country Business Award – Hospitality and Leisure – shortlisted

Jun 2016 Country Homes and Interiors Magazine

"Thank you very much for entering the My Country Business Award – Hospitality and Leisure."

"We are delighted to let you know that you have been shortlisted in this category. The shortlist will be announced this week on our social platforms, and the winner will be announced in early July."

CONGRATULATIONS – MEDIA COVERAGE – LUXURY RENTAL MARKET

Multi-Award-Winning Interior Designer.

Kerrie Griffin

PROFESSIONALS – MEDIA COVERAGE – LUXURY RENTAL MARKET

I have been designing award-winning interiors for over twenty years. I most recently have won **Cheshire Interior Designer of the Year** in the Prestige Central England Awards in **November 2020**, along with **Interior Design Specialist of the Year in the Manchester & Northwest England Prestige Awards in January 2021**.

This joins a long list found in the back of my book.
I have also been painting for thirty-five years. I created a company called The Interior Co over twelve years ago with a passion for helping make houses feel like homes. I saw a market gap to assist people, from planning for a smooth execution to supplying everything needed for their project.

AWARD-WINNING – REVENUE – INCREASE PROPERTY VALUE

Kerrie and her daughter Jasmin

I am currently working out of Cheshire on my twenty-fifth collection, which is out now. On my website www.theinteriorco.co.uk, you can browse through all of my designs, along with my exclusive collections selected by me. There's everything from furniture, lighting, accessories, and my very own original art, gifts and dowsing, plus some antique finds that I up-cycle or reupholster to create unique pieces for your amazing homes.

If you would like me to give you an award-winning look, please contact me at kerrie@theinteriorco.co.uk.

AWARD-WINNING - REVENUE - INCREASE PROPERTY VALUE

I have been to many holiday cottages over the years, and they were not very nice; a lot of them were damp and musty with old, tired furniture; I remember doing the gardening and watering the plants at a few; they were so unloved.

I wanted to create an experience like a hotel in a holiday let, and this became a money-spinner sooner than I thought, earning in the region of £32,000 per year. It was fully booked for six months within two weeks of opening.

I was a winner on Sunday 3rd March 2014 of the initiative Small Business Sunday, created by **Dragon's Den's Theo Paphitis,** and was recently a finalist in the **Inspirational Mother Awards; Interior Design Specialist, January 2021 Manchester;**
Interior Designer of the Year, November 2020, Cheshire;
Courage Award, November 2019 Positivity Awards. Additionally, I was the winner of **Highly Commended – Residential Interior Designer of the Year, NDA 2017**, selected by Linda Barker and Paul Smith.

AWARD-WINNING - REVENUE - INCREASE PROPERTY VALUE

I was also previously selected by **Rachel Elnaugh** from a previous **Dragon's Den** series. I was a finalist in two categories, **Business Woman of the Year** and **Rachel Elnaugh's Enterprise Award** in the finals of Free to **Network Business Awards in November 2013."**

Kerrie Griffin

REVENUE – INCREASE PROPERTY VALUE – BUSINESS FROM HOME

Kerrie outside the garage which is now Turtledove Hideaway.

DREAM – VISION – CREATE – REALITY – DEDICATION

I am thought of as a well-established interior designer and artist and I formed the company on the back of many years of combined experience in a wide range of industries, from building and construction to project management, full interior design, and soft furnishings, flooring, and all that fits in the middle.

My work has been featured in many interior magazines in Canada, Italy, Germany and many well-known English interior design magazines; see these in our section "Publicity."

Our staff and associates are fully qualified, experienced professionals within their sector with one goal: our clients' complete satisfaction.
We ensure that we understand our clients' needs so that each design reflects our clients' lifestyle and personal taste. Our in-house team, led by me, will create a visually harmonious design concept, and we also offer simple, clear, straightforward plans, which you can implement yourself if chosen.
In 2021 I will be starting a subscription-based membership site for all things interiors and business.

DREAM – VISION – CREATE – REALITY – DEDICATION

TESTIMONIALS

Rachele Biancalani
Italian Architect & Interior Designer March 2014

"I really love Kerrie's style because she uses a very natural mood combined with a more traditional style. Country meets wood; hills meet the sea; feathers meet paintings in Kerrie Griffin-Rogers' interiors. In my opinion, interior design is a sort of vocation, and she has it. Her sensibility leads her to always use the right colours and give the right vibe to every project. Furniture and accessories chosen and created by Kerrie are, in a single word: perfect!"

Claire Ray
Marketing Manager at Unique Home Stays

"Kerrie has truly worked her stylish magic on the Turtledove Hideaway; elegant sophistication and effortless romance combine to create an exceptional home indeed. Simple touches and careful attention to detail ensure that the overall effect is one of luxury and pure relaxation. I adore the popular Turtledove Hideaway, and the press attention and great booking levels we have generated for it since it joined the Unique Home Stay portfolio is testament to how attractive Kerrie's interiors are to both journalists and clients alike."

CREATIVE – HIGHLY RECOMMENDED – PROBLEM SOLVER

Debbie Jeffery
Property Journalist

"Kerrie has impeccable taste and a natural flair for making interiors look gorgeous and feel comfortable and welcoming. She is genuinely interested in finding what will work for each client and tailoring her skills to their needs. The result appears effortless."

Lisa Marsh
Banking Professional

Kerrie has made me more aware of what works and has given me the confidence to try different ideas; I wouldn't have done that before enlisting Kerrie.
I would highly recommend Kerrie; she has a great understanding of what you are trying to achieve and will work with you until you get the desired look you are hoping for. With extremely professional and excellent knowledge of her field, Kerrie comes highly recommended, and I will be using her services shortly."

CREATIVE – HIGHLY RECOMMENDED – PROBLEM SOLVER

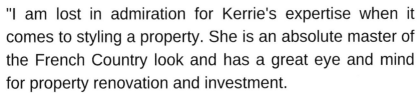

Alison Gibb
Interior Stylist and Writer

"I am lost in admiration for Kerrie's expertise when it comes to styling a property. She is an absolute master of the French Country look and has a great eye and mind for property renovation and investment.
She has helped me hugely in my recent search for the perfect home, gently reminding me all the time about what is important and what makes a property magical. I cannot wait to read this book and learn more from her."

Paula Woods
Freelance Journalist and Stylist

"Kerrie is a talented artist and interior designer I have been happy to feature in various interior magazines. Taking inspiration from the colours, seasons, and textures of nature, her signature look is timeless, restful, comfortable to live with, and always applied with a deft and knowledgeable hand."

CREATIVE – HIGHLY RECOMMENDED – PROBLEM SOLVER

TESTIMONIALS

Paul Wills
Principal Photographer at Willford Photographic.

"I have photographed Kerrie's work on several occasions for feature work for magazine covers, where she has displayed work for charitable events.

I find Kerrie's work visually appealing with a high standard of production values. She is, without doubt, a lovely, genuine, creative person, and it is a pleasure to know and work with her.

I would have no doubts about recommending Kerrie & wish her all the very best with the growing business."

CREATIVE – HIGHLY RECOMMENDED – PROBLEM SOLVER

Hayley Forrester
Shropshire

"Where do I start?! Kerrie first designed the interior for my mum's farmhouse: classy, tasteful and practical. So many people have commented about how gorgeous it looks. I moved into my own home and knew I was going to ask Kerrie to do the same. She has a true talent for interiors; your house is not complete unless she's done a consultation for you and I really mean this.

As well as a world-class interior designer, Kerrie is also a property developer and a practical person in nature. She looks at value-adding too."
"I'm so happy with her ideas for my upstairs and can't wait for her to see this in fruition when she designs the downstairs."

CREATIVE – HIGHLY RECOMMENDED – PROBLEM SOLVER

The Hall I created was featured in various Magazines.
Michelle P
Business Owner at Making the Shift

"Kerrie has an excellent eye for design. Her interior designs are stylish yet practical. She has a knack for creating beautiful living spaces that everyone covets. If you don't know where to start designing an interior space, I wouldn't hesitate to recommend using Kerrie for her vision and ideas."

CREATIVE – HIGHLY RECOMMENDED – PROBLEM SOLVER

My Feather paintings successfully finish the look from a garage to a boutique getaway, reflecting the chic, country style created.

My work can be found for sale on my website.

HIGHLY ARTISTIC – COMMERCIAL ARTIST – FEATHERS

MY STORY

What started as a showroom for my interior design company became a real money maker. I was forty-six years old and a single mother of two, struggling to pay the large mortgage on my home.

My husband had left us – I had no job and very little money to pay the bills. So, I started an interior design business called. The Interior Co began by selling my possessions to buy stock. I started by inviting friends to my home, and then word-of-mouth had me quickly being asked to do house parties. It wasn't long before people from a wider area wanted to buy my style and my choice of furnishings and vintage finds I had acquired along the way.
So, I finally went online, showcasing my many varied style products.

One summer's day, I was sitting outside, painting, when the rain started to come down. I pulled my chair and easel into the open garage, thinking, "Wouldn't it be great to have this space just for work, so I don't disturb everything in the house? And I can leave all my things out so I can walk back in when I feel creative."

HIGHLY ARTISTIC – COMMERCIAL ARTIST – FEATHERS

MY STORY

With an investment of £10,000 and a vision of what it could be, my shed soon became a £3,200-a-month retreat for couples. I contacted Unique Home Stays, a company that markets only the most distinctive luxury accommodation for travellers.

They are very discerning when it comes to the properties they will represent, yet my converted shed was accepted into their unique property portfolio.

I can't say the rest has been clear sailing – there are several hurdles to overcome when setting up a holiday let. Let's just say the sails got a little windblown, but in the end, we sailed on into harbour.

TIP
I was already using the building as an office, for which I didn't need planning because I didn't have any employees. However, be warned, as soon as you have one employee, planning is required. So, I applied for a change of use to use it as a holiday let.

Unique Home Stays had already included it in their portfolio before I had planning approved, so I had to move fast. They loved it and wanted to use it as a couple's retreat.

PROFESSIONAL – EXCELLENT KNOWLEDGE – CREATIVE FLAIR

The look before I cut holes and inserted windows and a wood burner.

The same shot after I have finished.

PROFESSIONAL – EXCELLENT KNOWLEDGE – CREATIVE FLAIR

This is how the structure was left for a few years.

How I did it

First, I saved shed loads of money! At first, I didn't have a penny to my name. I was left with nothing but a huge mortgage to pay and no job.

I sold everything I didn't use or need and saved up £2,200 to buy the slate to put a roof on the building, as there was a blue tarpaulin stapled onto the eaves for about eighteen months, driving me crazy on a dark winter's night blowing around.

DESIGN – CREATE – ENJOY

Oh, the times I had to climb a ladder to staple parts back on after high winds! Although I could have used a cheaper option, I wanted to put a roof on the property which blended in with the main house, so it was in keeping.

I opted for Welsh slate; I wouldn't recommend using any of the Chinese or Spanish slates as they lose colour, and the £400 savings will not be worth it. Go for quality all the way, even if it costs more and takes longer. Savings can be made on unseen things. An overall cost for all building materials (doors, windows, boards, joists, insulation, plasterboard, etc.) and fire protection and bathroom equipment are all included in this price: £4,899.66

I put the roof on myself, saving over £1,000, which I could then spend on other items to push the project on more quickly. Google how to put on a slate roof; that's how I learned!

NO JOB – NO MONEY – LITTLE HOPE – NO ROOF – VISION

As I have already mentioned, I started a business some years ago, which I ran from the main house, but it had been so successful I needed to upsize and have a real space to work from, which inspired me. Being an interior designer and an artist, it had to resemble a home, as that is how I work most creatively. Owning a company selling interiors and clothing, I needed a backdrop for photographing products.

This seemed the most straightforward idea: convert the beautiful oak garage into a workspace.

NO JOB – NO MONEY – LITTLE HOPE – NO ROOF – VISION

Many builders told me it was impossible to put an upstairs in the garage as there wasn't enough head height.

I would love a house by the sea, so with that in mind, I used this space to design and create a peaceful beach-style retreat.

It took only four weeks to complete the structure and fit the bathroom, kitchen and flooring, etc. Let's say I was motivated by not having any money to pay my mortgage.

NEAT BUT PERFECT–SHARP STYLE–HUES OF GREYS

Enter everything you can to raise your profile, then send press releases to get some media coverage.

NO JOB – NO MONEY – LITTLE HOPE – NO ROOF – VISION

At first, I was just going for half the floor space upstairs as I wanted to keep the vaulted ceiling on at least half of the building; however, after doing the half, I realised I would gain more from the build in terms of space upstairs if we put the floor in the whole building. Once the floor was laid then the space started to become real, I decided to put a window in each end to let the light flood in and to be able to see the dramatic views over the fields from upstairs; it gave you a sense you really were in a hideaway. The day I put the windows in, it seemed to increase the floor space upstairs by double; the effect was immediate.

I put tongue and groove on both apex gable ends running horizontally, as I wanted the room to look wider. Then I painted it white to seal the wood in an undercoat to give it a good base.

I then rolled the grey paint over the top with a small foam roller as they splatter less. For something as precise as this, you need the smaller roller; it missed the grooves from the tongue and groove, so it created the effect of white lines running through the grey, which looked fabulous, accentuating the width.

NO JOB – NO MONEY – LITTLE HOPE – NO ROOF – VISION

I painted the walls and woodwork, and the windows looked great painted in the same colour as the tongue and groove; it made the outside come in rather than putting a frame around the outside space.

I placed an apex poly cornice on the ceiling to finish where the plasterboard ended each side to tidy it up and painted it the same colour, giving it a contemporary feel. I packed the cavity full of insulation where the walls meet the roof, so it was completely sealed and draught free.

I then set the lights at regular intervals along both sides of the room lengthwise along the floor line so that when the lights are on, it gives the impression of the maximum width and length of the room.

It worked perfectly to create a peaceful, tranquil area to snooze the night away.

I had the electrician fit a remote so guests wouldn't have to get out of bed to switch the lights off – another little trick to make your guests feel extra special.

INCREASE FLOOR SPACE – ACCENTUATE WIDTH

TIP
If you want your narrow room to look broader, try putting your tongue and groove horizontally, which automatically gives the room width. In a low-ceiling-height room, use the downlighter lights about a foot higher than the floor and use them every two to three feet apart to give the illusion of expanding the floor area by double. The lighter it is, the bigger space feels.

I wanted to keep the open plan downstairs because there was nothing to gain by introducing walls which didn't need to be there. I needed a kitchen area, so I decided to put that at the back under the dropped eaves from the cat-slide roof at the rear, creating a cute, well-planned area for making myself a drink or lunch or washing my paintbrushes off. I found a company on the internet, which supplied top-quality, solid carcasses, then bought some doors from Door Swap.

The company that provided the carcasses also supplied the worktop and fitted this along with all the doors. The finish is superb, and by doing it this way, I managed to save hundreds of pounds, yet it looks costly and of the best quality.

LET LIGHT FLOOD IN – VISION

Let the energy flow

I love the worktops. Initially, I had ordered cream tiles to go with the cream worktop, but when they arrived, they looked a slightly different cream, so I went for the pearl colour, a lovely grey. And as the worktop had little specks of the same colour running through it, it brought the whole look together.

If it looked good on your colour board but didn't in real life, don't be afraid to change it out.

LET LIGHT FLOOD IN – VISION

I thought it would be great to put a bathroom in to avoid having to keep running into the main house and thought that if my teenage daughter had her friends' round, again instead of trashing my house, I would be able to offer them somewhere safe where they could let their hair down.

I put downlighters on the straight part of the wall so that when you were in bed, rather than blinding you, they gave a soft, low lighting effect creating yet again a visual look of space.

Downstairs I used a combination of tilting downlighters to highlight areas, and the linen and wood wall lights all switched from separate switches so areas could be closed off to the light, giving different effects of cosiness.

I made sure the bathroom was big enough to house a shower in case of sleepovers and created a wardrobe in there, too, as I didn't want to spoil the bedroom by taking too much space out of it by squeezing in fitted wardrobes. I wanted to create a feeling of space, which inspires me to work with a clearer head.

SOFTLY LIT INTERIORS – LINENS – NEUTRAL TILES

The space is fantastic as an office and for accommodation. Everything is kept tidy in boxes, and after I have painted a painting, they are hung on the wall so I can photograph them and get them online straight away.

I sew my Feathers of Italy labels into my clothing range when they arrive from Italy, then pack them ready to post to my customers. A building like this is so versatile in so many ways; you can turn it on and off as a holiday let when you feel like it; if you have family wanting to visit, but you need your own space, this is ideal.

TIP
Apply a soft colour to the walls, then paint the skirting slightly darker to edge the room. This will make the room look bigger. It pushes the walls back.

I chalked in several options to see where the kitchen and bathroom could be placed and how the stairs would work and be affected by where I put them. By chalking-out on the floor first, you can really see it in real time.

The stairs were my biggest nightmare, as once I had put them up, they totally overwhelmed the downstairs space, so I started looking into alternatives.

SOFTLY LIT INTERIORS – LINENS – NEUTRAL TILES

I looked at old vintage ladders, but they were all too short.

I go to the auction houses regularly, and the local auction room had a sale the following week on Monday.

I could barely wait to get it home before transforming it with The Little Green Paint Company's Slaked Lime Deep intelligent eggshell then rubbing it back on all the ridges and edges to create a vintage staircase. It took up barely any space at all, and as it was, an open staircase.

At a later date, when we applied for Building Regs to turn it into the holiday let, the ladder had to be replaced with something safe – a custom-made staircase with gaps between each step to create the same feeling of space again as the ladder.

I painted the steps in a dark grey to match the sidewalls upstairs, for the staircase to lead you up to the colour upstairs without it being a shock.

Once I had rubbed out and re-chalked several layout plans on the floor, I decided to put the bathroom at the back of the space to the right, keeping the front area as big as possible to create space illusion when you first enter.

The beams were really weathered because there had been no roof on the oak frame for several years, then a tarpaulin stapled on which kept blowing off in high winds. I wanted the floor to blend in, so I chose Quick Steps washed driftwood in soft grey to create the feeling of space.

TIP
By keeping an open plan, you create a bigger space, after all, this is a double garage.

WELL-PLANNED LAYOUT

I decided to put in a real fire, so I chose the Dimples Westcott 5 wood burner as I often popped into the house for an hour or so and needed the fire to keep alight safely without me there. The hardest thing was choosing the flue, as there were so many on the market and all at such different prices varying from £600 to £900.

UNIQUE PIECES – OPEN-PLAN HOUSES

A gorgeous wood burner is on a lot of must-haves
when finding a romantic retreat.

I phoned quite a few companies, and Flue Supplies
was so helpful and knew straight away all the parts I
needed to make a successful flue for a wooden
building. As we had put the window on the gable end,
and I chose to put the log burner in the middle of that
wall, we had to create a bend in the flue.

TIP
Invest in a wood burner. It makes the room cosy and
is safe.
It's also a must with some holiday-let guests – it's
on their tick list.

Not bad roofing for a girl.

I got some labour in to help with the heavy work. I roofed the building the year before in slate with a friend (after watching how to do it on YouTube!) whilst up the ladder in the rain in January with soaking wet jeans, so I knew the building inside-out. First, I stripped off the timber to the side elevation, which was nice and weathered, and I filled in the left-hand side garage opening with it, so it looked like it had always been there. I then used an old stable door from a previous overhaul as the main door and bought three windows from a friend for £50 each

WATCH YOUTUBE TO LEARN ROOFING – WELSH SLATE

They had them made, but they came the wrong size; it didn't matter as we were creating new gaps. We then put the door and window in the open space it had created, we put in the two windows which overlooked a country cottage garden area to let in south-facing light and gave an inspiring view, and then boarded back up the area with new treated weatherboard planks from ETC at Oswestry, which cost £65. These have been up several years now, and you cannot tell the difference between the oak and the treated wood. But, over time, these won't last as long as the oak.

Next, the floor went in, and the windows upstairs and then we insulated the whole roof space, including the cat-slide area to the back to retain maximum heat once the fire was lit.

WATCH YOUTUBE TO LEARN ROOFING – WELSH SLATE

KITCHEN

Make a home guests want to return to. Go the extra mile.

I designed the kitchen with a curved door to the right as I didn't want any sharp edges making the space look smaller, and I wanted it to flow towards the bathroom entrance.

The carcasses and worktops came from Vision Kitchen Design in Oxford. The worktop is called Mistral. I chose to use them because they were a small, independent company that really cared about their products.

WATCH YOUTUBE TO LEARN ROOFING — WELSH SLATE

They came to fit the whole lot, including the bathroom's worktop (which was an off-cut he did for a bacon butty!), making the curved edges and ridges for draining on site. It was great to watch it transform from pieces of stone to worktops. I chose the biscuit worktop to make the kitchen float into the room space and not stand out in any way. The worktop had little specks of the same colour running through, so it brought the whole look together. The fitter who came fitted the doors on the carcasses and did a fantastic job. I now have a costly looking kitchen for a lot less money than if I had gone to a company that supplies the whole lot.

TIP
Try buying the carcasses from one company and the doors from another; surprisingly, you save pounds. Look for auctions and pop into your local kitchen showroom to see if they are ripping any out which have been on display, often at a fraction of the cost.

SAVE MONEY – NO SHORTCUTS

BATHROOM

I built two drywalls for the bathroom and then got the electrician to do the first fix. I used Sarah, one of my customers, and she was brilliant. She was on my wavelength and knew just what I wanted to achieve. Please don't underestimate the price of a full-fix electrician; get several quotes and make sure they are registered. Your guest's safety is your responsibility.

The walls were all plaster boarded, then the bathroom suite and the floor were ready to be laid. I chose luxurious porcelain tiles in a mink colour to give the feeling of warmth to the small bathroom.

CLEVER BUYING – CLEVER PLANNING

BATHROOM

Because it's a small area, you can afford an elegant tile. I tiled the walls and floor in the same tile. It was challenging cutting the tiles, as they are so tough, and I had to buy a diamond cutter which was about £50. I laid all the tiles and a friend cut them.

I bought a great sink from Victoria Plumb and some taps – each was £69, the shower was £149 including a base tray, and the curved sliding door was £149. The toilet was eco and was £89 with the seat being £12 from Ikea.

I made the washstand to house the sink from three-by-twos and wooden planks. To make the shelves' spacing, I got some of the rattan baskets I sell and set them out to determine where the shelves needed to be before drilling and screwing together at the right height allowances for sliding them in and out.

I then painted it in the same colour as the woodwork. I then painted the walls and ceiling in Slaked Lime Dark emulsion and the woodwork in Slaked Lime Deep by The Little Green Paint Company, and this subtle difference in shade really does work, creating a subtle contrast. Sarah, the electrician, came back and fitted the wooden and linen light fittings, which then started to bring the look together.

LIMEWASHED WASHSTAND – SIMPLE SINK

BATHROOM

I could barely wait to get the furniture in; in fact, she helped me drag the chateau chair upstairs to see what it would look like. What a nightmare it turned out to be as it was so heavy. Every way we tried it; it just wouldn't fit. Eventually, after several cups of tea and hair being pulled out in disbelief, it didn't fit. I turned it on its side, then in 180-degree turns. It was in place, positioned in front of the window looking across the fields with a table with a lamp and book at the side and a cosy blanket draped over the arm with "Home" written on it. It really gives you a sense of spending afternoons sitting up there reading or watching nature.

TIP
Try making a washstand, it's fairly simple. This cost me about £20 plus he let me have the worktop offcut for a bacon butty, about £1.

LIMEWASHED WASHSTAND

Whilst she was wiring up upstairs, my solid wood painted bed arrived from Colour Supplies, but when it came, I changed my mind about its position in the room (as I am prone to do), so I decided to cut about eight inches off the legs to give more head height when sitting on the bed.

The final layout works entirely open-plan; it's bigger than I expected it to look with all the careful planning of furniture to maximise the floor space.

I put in the wall for the bathroom, and when the shower tray arrived, it was ten centimetres bigger. But as we were working against the clock, I had to move the wall overnight before the builder came back to fit the bathroom the next day.

I re-used the old stable door repainted (which had been taken from my house when I renovated it) and bought a new frame for £40.

Making the washstand was quick and straightforward and cost about £25.

The light fittings were only £43 each. I used as many as I could fit in to give lots of light.

FLEXIBILITY – DISTRESSED - VINTAGE LADDER

Add a desk for those who may need to do a little work;
Internet isn't always a must but helps.

QUIRKY ACCESSORIES

I didn't plaster the walls to cut costs; I just painted the plasterboard.

I made the wardrobe doors in the bathroom from two packs of tongue and groove. I laid them on a flat surface and knocked about four together so they fit inside one another; I then braced them at the back with two horizontal pieces of wood (two-by-one), then painted them before hanging with some black hinges to give a cottage feel.

Paint Colours – Why Neutrals?

I wanted to create a great open living area and use neutral paint colours alongside the beautiful oak frame of the building to make it look like it had always been there. The result is fantastic.

Choice of Materials

I chose wood for the floor, as I wanted it to be practical, living in the country, walking in and out with possible chickens, visiting children and dogs. I liked the grey colour to blend in with the weathered grey oak of the building's internal frame.

I chose tiles in the bathroom in a dark tone to give a warm cosy feel to the room, and I decided that porcelain would give the room a luxury.

BARGAINS – PRACTICAL CHOICES

TIP
A wood floor is practical for country living and longevity. Use the best quality materials on the things that really matter, like the roof, worktops and floors.

WEATHERED OAK – PORCELAIN TILES

I had put two fence panels up to keep the rain out of the building's front whilst I worked on putting the floor in. Routine practice is to get the building watertight first, but my schedule was tight, just four weeks.

SCHEDULES – OAK – WATERPROOF – WELSH SLATE

RESULTS

House on the prairie style bedroom

A space to sit and contemplate,
read or even write a book!

SCHEDULES – OAK – WATERPROOF – WELSH SLATE

I had to create a feeling of space.

I was in a real dilemma as I knew it would look great to have the log burner with the chimney running inside right through the roof and looking up to a mezzanine bedroom, but if I did that, the only place I could have the staircase would be in the middle of the room, cutting it in half.

I was not in a comfortable position. I decided that, although it would look amazing, it was a false economy. I needed the bedroom space to be bigger, and I wanted to put the staircase over to one side as near to the right-hand side as possible to give the feeling of space.

MEZZANINE STAIRCASE OPEN PLAN

The first half of the floor down now, ready to cut out a hole to fit a window in.

I live by the Interiors rule look – glamorous at all times. The poor joiner kept banging his head on the chandelier he had to work around! See page 18 for the finished result. This was to become the upstairs-seated area overlooking the rolling countryside.
Ok, so do I leave half the room to the eaves or board up all of it to give more bedroom space?

MEZZANINE – STAIRCASE – CHANDELIER

Making an entrance welcoming.

MEZZANINE – STAIRCASE – CHANDELIER

PLANNING PROBLEMS

One morning I heard a bang at the door. It was 8:30 a.m., and I was still in my pyjamas.

They were standing on my doorstep: The Building Regulations, Planning and Council Tax officers. They said, "We want to see in there," and pointed to the garage.

I asked, "What for?"
They said, "It's being used as a shop."
"News to me," I said.

I thought they were joking and laughed. They said, "Who have you upset?" It was like a film, with the heavy mob turning up. Anyway, I grabbed a coat and opened the door; they were flabbergasted and said, "It's a cottage, you don't have planning, who lives here?"

I said, "No one. I did it as an office," but a magazine had decided to feature it, mentioning that it had a kitchen and a bathroom.

One of them started climbing the ladder to see upstairs. To his delight, he said, "It has a bed too." It was like bloody Goldilocks and the Three Bears, "This bed is too soft, this bed is too hard" – anyway back to the story in hand. They said, "We have reason to believe you are using it as a B&B."

MEZZANINE – STAIRCASE – CHANDELIER

I said, "Isn't a B&B attached to your house?"
They said, "It's close enough."

I said, "Do me a favour, flush the toilet and turn the taps on, oh and whilst you're all at it, follow me outside to see the waste pipe protruding through the side of the wall, and you will see we have no drainage or sewerage connected, so how can it be fit for habitation?" at the moment.
I said, "But it's a bloody good idea! How do I apply for planning permission?"
They said, "You probably won't get it as it's retrospective planning."
I replied, "I'll take my chance. What do I have to do?"
They said, "It's expensive."
I said, "How much?"
They said, "Around £350."
I said, "Show me the forms," and I literally followed them back to the offices with my application and cheque in my hand! What fuelled me was partly anger that the neighbours had been so interfering in trying to stop me having a holiday let for myself when they already had one, and also when someone says to me, "it can't be done," I make it happen.

MEZZANINE – STAIRCASE – CHANDELIER

The Building Regs guy came around, all high and mighty, threatening to cut big holes in the plasterboard to see if the insulation was the right thickness, but I had read somewhere that this wasn't necessary if you had photographic evidence which could be used. If you have photos of the ongoing progress, some planning authorities may accept this, and others could still ask you to cut holes in your walls to make sure what thickness your insulation is.

I questioned him and asked for a second opinion from his boss. I had had a fantastic piece of advice from a features editor to ask so many questions that they will be glad to leave. Well, it worked very successfully! I fired one question after another at him until he said there was no need to cut big holes in the walls, he was also more lenient on a few things after that, and we agreed on which works were to be carried out.

They were accommodating, unlike my first meeting with the council mafia, and within a few weeks, all work was completed and signed off. It was a bit hairy, which is not an ideal situation, but my life seems to be full of these types of happenings. I live off pressure anyway.

PLANNING – NEIGHBOURS

The Building Regs inspection was booked for the morning of my first houseguests' arrival day. They were arriving at 4 p.m.; the Building Regs officer was due at 11 a.m. Thank God I wasn't there, as I may have buckled under the stress. My friend Richard was there to greet them and showed them the alterations we had made at their request, and they signed it off there and then.

I then arrived home, welcomed the guests and opened one of many bottles of champagne to celebrate. Any excuse! I always say celebrate at every corner of a project; then it goes quicker. Put the floor in – a bottle of champagne is cracked open. Doors in – champagne to celebrate, you get the picture!

TIP
Problems with planners? When they arrive, bombard them with questions! Don't be rude or cocky. It will not go in your favour if you are.

PROBLEMS – ACTIONS – RESULTS

WHAT DO PEOPLE WANT?

In general, our visitors are looking to stay in a quiet, rural location away from it all but with the comforts of a five-star hotel. They want to try something different, something that's a million miles from what they do in their everyday life. People really enjoy getting back to nature and experiencing a more relaxed kind of holiday, but we all like a bit of luxury.

Holidays are so precious; we don't get enough time to holiday, and we want to make the most of it in luxurious accommodation. We almost want to combine all the best bits of life – great food, a good night's sleep, peace and quiet, cooking outdoors. Don't forget to supply a BBQ; they are not just for summer, but romance and adventure at any time of year, wrapping up warm and having a BBQ in the winter.

Believe me, it is very romantic if you are on holiday and there are pretty lights outside. All this is hard to come by in their everyday lives. Unique Home Stays holiday let experts came on the scene to search the country for unusual and exciting properties you would never find yourself, let alone be able to stay in. The company has a unique way of tracking down the properties that aren't on the market and that no one knows about.

PROBLEMS – ACTIONS – RESULTS

To stay in something like this is a real honor – you feel special, and we like that. Feeling considerably more special than usual is the number one must-have.

When deciding on your project, whether it be a shepherd's hut or converting your stable, garage, or outhouse, it's not just a question of renovating a building or putting up a structure and expecting it to do very well. There are many other things to consider. You need a great setting. Location, location, location! You need an idea for what you want to do, and then you need to create something unique, something no one else has. I feel that mine is unique and memorable due to the fantastic layout and the story behind it, i.e., this was a double garage, and I used my skills as an interior designer to put everything in its place to create a cosy but spacious property.

Investing in professionals like an interior designer will pay dividends. I interviewed an extensive range of my guests, and 99.9 percent said they chose the accommodation for its interior styling. By working with an interior designer, you won't make any wrong decisions. Money will be saved, not wasted, and you will create something unique and special.

By quoting the interior designer's name or "designed by an interior designer," it already builds certain credibility to your project. When you then have the product, the only thing left to do is to market your property.

CHOOSING A LETTING AGENT

At this point, you can choose to do it yourself or invest in using the professionals. I decided to use what I considered perfect for my property: a holiday letting company specialised in unusual and exciting properties with many years of experience and lots of social media and media coverage.

I do everything in threes, so this was no exception. Choose three reputable companies to come out and view the let; get their knowledge of the market, what people are looking for and to whom it would appeal; then ask if they would change anything and get their rates and suggested forecasted incomes; then start by the process of elimination.

I thought at the time when I had invited three of the top holiday companies around, "Why is Unique Home Stays the only company asking for a fee?" But when they arrived, I understood. They are passionate about their properties, knowledgeable, and they mean business. If yours is the one for them, you will know straight away. They don't hold back. They offer realistic, constructive criticism and provide on-the-spot facts and figures and, of course, excellent marketing. They have one staff member assigned to your property, and she is there to get you the maximum amount of press coverage. After all, if you read about Turtledove Hideaway in the Sunday Times, you will want to stay there. We have been in seven national magazines, three of which were in Europe and one as far away as Canada, and five national newspapers.

The £150 fee we initially paid to Unique Home Stays was worth every penny. If you don't get accepted, you would understandably feel it was wasted, but take it this way – this consultancy fee for them telling you how to improve it will be well worth the £150 and will be paid back tenfold if you take their advice.

PROBLEMS – ACTIONS – RESULTS

With a bumper year ahead predicted for the UK luxury holiday rentals market, Claire Ray of Unique Home Stays offers a few pointers.

What are the up-sides to a premium holiday rental over a luxury hotel with facilities on tap? Why book a hotel room when you can book a whole house and get so much more for your money? The overriding benefit of a private rental over a hotel stay is privacy, seclusion and freedom (not to mention the bed-to-bath ratios!). With Unique Home Stays as well as receiving all the little luxuries offered by boutique hotels (fluffy bathrobes, luxury toiletries, concierge/in-house chef on request), guests can luxuriate in privacy with a range of facilities ranging from swimming pools, cinema rooms, saunas, hot tubs and more.

It ultimately depends on the party's requirements and personal tastes. Hectic schedules and busy lives can often mean little time to truly relax and take time out as a family. Variety is vital – choosing a location with plenty to do on the doorstep is essential.

PROBLEMS – ACTIONS – RESULTS

Opting for a property with on-site facilities (private indoor pool sauna, games room) is a tremendous failsafe, particularly with the unpredictable UK weather. If you are planning to go away with a large family group with lots of different ages, it's nice to have the option of a rental that comprises two houses, to allow freedom for families to spread out and relax as they wish.

What VIP extras can prospective holidaymakers expect these days from a luxury rental?

We encourage our property owners to exercise individuality and character in everything – from the well-thumbed books on the shelves to the carefully chosen artwork on the walls and their choice of homemade cakes and glasses of fizz on arrival. VIP extras can range from pre-requisites such as luxury bed linen and towels and freshly cut flowers to hot tubs, his and her Hunter wellies, and afternoon tea on arrival.

When are the best times of the year to secure an off-peak deal – is it better to wait until the last minute before booking?

The low season is October – March (excluding October half term, Christmas, New Year and February half-term).

PROBLEMS – ACTIONS – RESULTS

It's a good idea to have a good range of properties on your shortlist to compare and contrast potential options. Some agencies might offer last-minute deals; it depends on the company, but worth checking!

If the rental experience falls short of your expectations – what is the best course of action?
Flag any issues straight away to your rental company – don't leave it until the end of your break as they will and should be able to rectify any problem as quickly as possible. Send an e-mail too, so you have something in writing that logs your complaint.

Specialising in remarkable private holiday houses that simply can't be found elsewhere, Unique Home Stays holds the key to beautiful private homes which are truly unique and breath-taking, exceeding expectations every step of the way.
Their discerning clients expect a luxurious escape when they book with us, but as well as an indulgence, they crave a holiday experience that will linger in the memory when their hard-earned downtime has long passed. Our aim is to exceed expectations every step of the way; for our owners, our clients and ourselves, 'good, average, nice' simply won't suffice.

PROFESSIONALS – MEDIA COVERAGE

For more information, contact them directly, but one thing to be wary of: my plan was to always do it myself after a few years as the commission was around 30 percent of sales, not sustainable forever. I had named my holiday let The Artists Retreat. They changed it and publicised it. When relationships broke down, they linked my property to an entirely different property in another part of the country, misleading past clients. I have asked them to remove it lots of times, and they refused. So, either stick to your name or market your property yourself. You won't get as many bookings, but it will be guaranteed you won't be pulled over a barrel with a gun to your head if you leave. I loved working with Unique Homestays. We were fully booked, but this kind of behaviour, in my mind, is unacceptable.

TIP
Get three holiday companies around and compare what they all say, then make your decision, use your SWOT analysis here (strengths, weaknesses, opportunities, and threats).

The character of the barn has been retained, giving a relaxed country feel. I did this by exposing and keeping as much of the timber frame on show as possible. The brick wall, which holds the oak frame, was supported around the base of the room.

This has immediately increased the value of the main house by £30,000, with no bookings but, as a business, I am told by Unique Home Stays that they will achieve £32,000 in revenue per year and with a few years under your belt of bookings you can achieve a return of over 100k added value.

The property shares the same drive and is relatively close to the main house, but neither encroaches on each other's space.

A WARM WELCOME AWAITS YOU

There was an old toilet and sink already there, so drainage and sewage were already connected, but they were poor and needed replacing, and a new manhole cover was required as an inspection point. This cost £650. I had to get a digger in and dig the old pipes up and replace them. It all had to be landscaped anyway at this point. If I had ignored this issue, it would have been costly later down the line, including having to close temporarily.

INSURANCE

'Public liability insurance is required, and most sites will require planning even if it's within the curtilage of the garden unless you're planning a pop-up for less than twenty-eight days. We'd always suggest getting the advice of a planning consultant.'

I took out a buildings and contents insurance policy with the B&B and the holiday let attached to the main house's buildings and contents. This was the cheapest way of insuring it with NFU.

A WARM WELCOME AWAITS YOU

MORTGAGE

Holiday home mortgages are a different proposition from buy-to-let. A holiday home-to-let lender and assessment of the property's value will have to determine the likelihood and frequency of rental periods throughout the year to calculate mortgage affordability. This will have to be quantified by a letter with predicted figures from a rental agent.

TAXES

Check with your local council. I was in Wales, and they won't charge council tax or rates for the first two years. (Currently, this is exempt in Wales for rural properties.)

BUILDING REGULATIONS

You will need building regulations for your let to make sure it is up to standards. The cost was £330, although they all differ.

PLANNING PERMISSION

General guidelines to avoid planning permission or tick all of their boxes:
The ridge height of the building should be no more than four metres.

A WARM WELCOME AWAITS YOU

THE LEGAL BITS

The building should be behind the front line of your house.
It should be five metres away from the house.
It should be two metres away from any boundary, i.e., neighbours, road, etc.
It should not be in a conservation area.
Height should be no more than four metres, and the square footage must be less than thirty square metres.

Planning permission and building regulations are required for a holiday let, as new building regulations are now in place concerning new guidelines for insulation values. Local authorities promote and encourage the change of use to holiday lets because it is good for local employment and encourages tourism into the area.
I needed Building Regs to bring the building up to standard. This depends on if you already have a structure and just need to convert or build from scratch. If you're not sure which to apply for – granny annexe or holiday let – it's worth spending some time looking into the benefits and pitfalls in each scenario. I also do a SWOT analysis on everything – strengths, weaknesses, opportunities, and threats – including men!

THE LEGAL BITS

If it's a holiday let you really want to do, then always contact your council business team they are essential and not many people know there is free help for building your business.

Interior by Kerrie Griffin - The Interior Co

HEIGHT – PLANNING – BUILDING REGS

IS IT ALL WORTH IT?

Will you get rich?

Is this all worth it, and how much money could you make?

Before you start, it's worth thinking about your motives for letting out space in your home or garden to guests.

It can be a bit of a minefield working out planning or tax obligations, and your insurance costs are likely to rocket.

This is because there is no one-size-fits-all option. Some people may be able to get away with minimal changes, but others will have to stump up a substantial amount of money. Equally, many people rent out charming spaces, some just a few metres wide, from £650 for a weekend to £2,000 a week or £100,000 a year.

A specialist website that handles converted timber shacks says it is struggling to keep up with demand. Unique Home Stays lists thirty-seven two-person boltholes, around half of which are located in popular tourist areas.

In my mind, if it's quirky, all the better. If you can fit a bed in and bathroom, great, rent it out! Some of the cutest places are the small ones; don't worry if you think yours is too small.

INCOME — EXPECTATIONS

HINTS &TIPS?

Once you have a project in mind, check to see if there is anything on the market to compare like-for-like and what they are getting in rental income.

Talk to a rental agent and ask them what type of properties are renting well and what they are looking to take on in the next six months, i.e., what is trending at their agency, if they need love nests or boltholes away from the cities.

Don't ignore their advice; I repeat, do not disregard their advice! So, if they are asking for love nests for two but yours would make a tremendous three-bedroom holiday let, and you know best because you think the rental income will be more, that isn't the case if you can't rent it out.

 Ask the agents what their expectations are of the finish, i.e., luxury or basic or somewhere in between. If you supply good quality fittings and furnishings, you will definitely reap a better return.

QUALITY – LUXURIOUS – REVIEWS

Top tip moan:

What annoys me is when people decide to create a beautiful room or building, and they build or renovate it to a really high standard, then they paint it magnolia because they don't know what to do with the interior then chuck in a load of either unloved ex furniture from their main house or flat-pack Ikea.

Your let should contain the same, if not better than what you have in your home, it should be an experience you want to repeat.

Employing an interior designer for as little as £1200 can totally make the difference between you renting your property and being fully booked or it is empty.

If you want to save money, you can, for instance, skimp on tiles because there is a massive difference in the market. Just opt for a deeper colour; they look more expensive. However, you can't skimp on the quality of sofas, linens, accessories and toiletries. If, for instance, you supply Molton Brown, you will attract a different clientele than if you provide, for example, M & S brand.

QUALITY – LUXURIOUS – REVIEWS

There's nothing wrong with it, but you just need to understand the fundamental rule, when people stay away from home, they expect better! But on the other hand, be sensible. My let is charging between £380 and £500 per short let, so I can't supply Jo Malone.

I can get better feedback from happy clients with DKNY dressing gowns and Osprey towels from TK Maxx at massively reduced prices and still get the luxurious look that commands fabulous reviews.

This is why it's all worth it; when you get an amazing review, it puts a smile on your face and fills a tiny space in your heart; plus, I have met the most amazing people; I have shared stories and even wine and nibbles. It's possibly the most rewarding thing, apart from when I see someone's smiling face when I have finished their interior, or they have purchased a painting from me.

EXPECTATIONS – QUALITY – LUXURIOUS

IF YOU GET A BAD REVIEW

It's only one person's opinion, so don't let it upset you. If you keep getting bad reviews, there is obviously something terribly wrong. I have had one bad review saying I had no cheese grater or weighing scales. Well, strike me down! It wasn't on the list of must-haves from the holiday let agents anyway, but I reacted. I bought both, even though no one else would ever use them. It's about taking constructive or even vindictive criticism with open arms and knowing what to react to and what not to. Remind yourself of all the happy customers by reading your reviews and you will be feeling more positve in no time.

"Perfect"
We had a lovely stay here over our three nights. The cottage was perfect for everything we needed and an excellent base for exploring the area. Thanks, Kerrie, for all the little touches and for making us feel so welcome.

EXPECTATIONS – QUALITY – LUXURIOUS

Before embarking on your project, make a list of things you need. See if you can use anything reclaimed where possible. Cost everything up, i.e.:

Building regulations – £330

Planning permission – £300

Roof – £2,200

All flooring – £1,800

Work for building regs – £1,100

Lighting/electrics – £1,800

Quality furniture – £5,000

Bathroom – £1,500

Kitchen – £2,000

Kitchen equipment – £440

Decoration/paint – £250

Accessories – £700

Soft furnishings – £900

Interior Designers – £3,200

Builder –£10,000

Joiner – £2,300

Labour – £2,500

Materials – £4,900.

(This does not include paint, kitchen and appliances, floor coverings or furniture and tiles.)

BUILDER – DESIGNER – JOINER

COSTS: DO YOUR FIGURES

When you have compiled your list, add another third to it, if not half, and you will be about there with your figures if anything goes wrong.

At this point, it is worth deciding on your list based on potential income versus value added to your property, and if at that point the figures sort of stack up and you have passion in your belly, just do it.

FURNITURE – ACCESSORIES

HOW TO MAKE YOUR BUSINESS STAND OUT

It's all in the detail.

In these tough economic times, we must offer a little more than everyone else does. It doesn't take much to go one step further; you must offer something a little extra to stand out from the crowd. When I go away, time is precious, and everything has to be perfect. I want my accommodation to be the same or better than at home, not worse. Why would we pay someone to have worse than what is at home? We want to be treated and spoilt.

IMPRESSIONS – QUALITY – QUIRKY –

HOW TO MAKE YOUR BUSINESS STAND OUT

TOP TIPS

Top tips for a perfect holiday let and lots of repeat customers and fantastic comments.

FIRST IMPRESSIONS are of utmost importance. Ensure your entrance/drive to the property is well maintained, lawns mowed, flowers in pots, bay trees on either side of the door, clean front door, clean windows, and front entrance is clean and tidy. Make sure the house, cottage (shed!) is warm and smells nice and has fresh flowers near the entrance to welcome guests.

FLUFFY NEW TOWELS (If they tire, throw them out; they are essential for the luxury vote.)

GOOD QUALITY LINENS in the bedroom, lounge and kitchen. Yes, even oven gloves and tea towels matter. If anything is stained, throw it away to keep your standards high.

SPOTLESS – Make sure the property is spotless. If you wouldn't stay in it, no one else will.

ARRIVAL MEET AND GREET – Make them feel your home is their home, for a few days at least.

FRESH – ORGANIC – FEATHER DUVETS

Ask if they have plans and suggest things to do and places to eat. Most people like information and hints and tips on what to do. I always offer to book tables at local restaurants and pubs, provide taxi services, reserving them for my clients, and giving my guests my mobile number and suggest that they text me if they need options of where to go or just a simple walk and directions. It's like a personal assistant being at the end of the phone.

HOME BAKING – My daughter always bakes cakes for the guests, dusts with icing sugar, and leaves them in a beautiful glass cake dome.

INTERESTING AND QUIRKY – Try to stock the property with some lovely, quirky objects or talking pieces and excellent quality china. My cottage appeals as a love nest for couples, so I put some beautiful Emma Bridgewater mugs which say, "Last night I dreamed about," and on the bottom, they say, "You." Cute and quirky, they notice.

MAGAZINES AND BOOKS – Leave an excellent quantity of exciting books, and if your property has been in any magazines, leave them in the property.

FLUFFY TOWELS – LUXURIOUS ACCESSORIES

FRESH LOCAL PRODUCE – I bought some chickens and left organic eggs in a bowl on the worktop with a little note saying, "I hope you enjoy our eggs; love Megan and Harry (my chickens' names). Do pop over to see us in the garden." Also, if I'm away, I ask the guests to feed the chickens. They love it.

FRESH FLOWERS AND CANDLES – Leaving fresh flowers for your guests is a personal touch. Most of my guests' comments refer to how welcoming they are. If there isn't an overlap of guests, I bring them into the house to enjoy. I always add greenery from the garden to bulk out my display. Candles are a lovely touch. I always leave about ten extra tea lights under the sink so they can refill themselves.

Always buy good quality candles. I like to light a few whilst I am cleaning the cottage, so it smells nice for the arrivals.

FLUFFY TOWELS – LUXURIOUS ACCESSORIES

Organic eggs go down a treat with guests.

FLUFFY TOWELS – LUXURIOUS ACCESSORIES

HOW IT STARTED

I initially wanted to get some private space away from my home where clients could visit me to see my work as an interior designer and artist. It was all getting a bit too much – having people in my house.

I felt overwhelmed and without a penny in hand, as my now ex-husband had emptied the bank accounts, shut us out of his life and left us to fend for ourselves in the middle of nowhere, leaving me with a massive mortgage with no income or money to support us.

I had to react fast. I sold my possessions to buy some stock, then sold the stock and bought more stock and so on, doubling my money each time until I had enough money to buy the roof tiles for my garage, now Turtledove Hideaway.

Once the garage was dry and clean, I was able to have house sales inside initially, which brought more income each time to buy a roll of loft insulation etc.

I had saved £2,000 to employ a joiner who put the floor in, sectioned off a space for the bathroom, insulated it, plaster boarded and put windows and doors in.

I had done enough to send some pictures to House Beautiful magazine, who said they would love to do an article on the garage once finished.

When they heard my story, companies came forward offering free products to put into the hideaway in exchange for free publicity. However, at this stage, we assured them that magazines, along with any press, could pull out at the last minute. This did not deter most of them.

On we went with the project. A friend and I did most of the internal work: fitting skirting boards, laying the oak floor, filling gaps, hanging oak doors and painting. Although it took ages to get the hang of the angles, which had to be cut for skirting boards wasting a lot of wood, luckily, most of the property base is brick because the oak frame sat on a four-brick high base.
I literally finished the day before the photo shoot. I filled the cottage with some sofas from the house and all my products from The Interior Co, it looked like a shop, but you could live in it – my kind of heaven.

FLUFFY TOWELS – LUXURIOUS ACCESSORIES

HOW IT STARTED

We already had bathroom and kitchen water to the property as there had been a fixing put in to wash the cars when it was built as a garage initially, but no drainage or sewerage, as it wasn't intended as a cottage, just my showroom.

Anyway, along came House Beautiful's Paula Woods, Interior Stylist, and the very best in interiors photographer, Lizzie Orm. Both said, "Oh my God, you can't use this as an office; this could start paying your mortgage. It's amazing! Who wouldn't want to come and stay in here?" The day progressed, and a champagne bottle was popped over lunch (see, I told you, any excuse!).

FLUFFY TOWELS – LUXURIOUS ACCESSORIES

They said I should contact the top holiday cottage companies, as my style was quirky and unique. The name Unique Home Stays was thrown into the conversation like a rag doll. I needed anything to get me out of the situation I was in and would consider anything, even having people in my property when I wanted to curl up in a ball and cry.

"Be brave," I thought. "It's fine; they will love it." Lizzie and Paula said it was fantastic and they should know as they see hundreds of properties each year.

The next day, I rang Unique Home Stays, I sent some pictures, and they immediately said, "We're interested." The stumbling block was £150. I had absolutely nothing left, not a penny; I struggled to buy petrol to get the children to school and feed them, let alone find £150 to pay on the off-chance they may take the property on. I sold a mirror to a friend at the ridiculous price of £150 just to get the money.

They came, they loved, and they conquered, and within forty-eight hours, I was offered a letting contract saying I could earn up to £32,000 per year.

FLUFFY TOWELS – LUXURIOUS ACCESSORIES

HOW IT STARTED

I was amazed and slightly dazed; was my awful luck finally changing? I signed and sent it back within minutes, checking the small print for the catch, but there wasn't one. They were investing in me, my look; it was terrific. The biggest shock was when I had my first booking a couple of days after going live, which was pretty quick. The children couldn't believe it. Mummy was clever, after all! And with my first payment, I bought a bottle of champagne and drank it with a friend. I think it's so important to not only celebrate but also share your triumphs with people!

We are now in our eighth year, February and March are fully booked, and we have had to create a B&B now to take all the people who want to experience a taste of my Interiors. We offer a boutique luxury B&B, offering Osprey towels, Ralph Lauren bed linen, and Molton Brown products. Breakfast includes organic eggs, bacon and sausages; all locally produced, I make freshly baked bread to leave for them. If I am busy, I pop to the bakery and grab a few cakes whilst I am there; it's the thoughtful touches that cost less than £10 that matter.

FLUFFY TOWELS – LUXURIOUS ACCESSORIES

Both businesses are a huge success due to the friendly, no-quibble approach I have to life.

Turtledove Hideaway is available to rent.

The Interior Co

Our online shop for all your Design and Interior needs.

NEW Virtual Interior Design, where we design your space from our desk to yours.

www.theinteriorco.co.uk info@theinteriorco.co.uk

Feathers of Italy Clothing available from.

www.feathersofitaly.co.uk

Artwork by Kerrie Griffin available from The Interior Co www.theinteriorco.co.uk

I can be reached on 07500930207

If you are interested in my incredible journey and want to find out more, I am writing a book called Bullshit and Half A Dozen Eggs, which is about deceit to success, which will inspire even the most nonchalant of people, due out in 2021.

DESIGN – CREATE – ENJOY – REAP REWARDS

What if you don't want to leave your dog at home. What is the market like and how much damage can I expect if I decide to take dogs?

Dog-Friendly Escapes

It's the heart-wrenching decision to leave your much-loved pet at the kennels. You don't see why they can't join you on your holiday too. Isn't that why we have a dog? To be our pal? To be by our side? Unique Home Stays say they have a real following for owners who have dogs but still expect luxury accommodation. They have a selection of unique, luxury, dog-friendly holiday properties across the UK.

Opening up to dogs brings a huge market of affluent dog owners prepared to pay a little more.

DOGS CHASE CATS — DOGS CHASE CATS

DOGS OR NO DOGS

You only get £50 extra per dog, but it does open you up to a whole extra bracket of otherwise unreachable holiday guests.

I decided to try it for a short period and said that if they didn't respect my property and things were destroyed, I would stop doing it. Luckily, so far, all dog visitors and owners have gone away happy and dogs' tails a-wagging.

Once you get over the initial thought of "Oh my God, my nice new items ... what if they destroy them?" and the dog-hair cleaning after the visit, then you should be happy to receive your dog-loving guests.

I put down wood in the ground floor area, and the bathroom is downstairs, so if the dog is filthy from a walk, they can hose it down in the shower. I have a real problem with dogs and dog hairs, muddy paws etc., so leave a specific dog towel if it's a rainy weekend. When they leave, everything is thoroughly cleaned, as I wouldn't want to find dog hair in my holiday let if I were staying. My rule of thumb consists of this: if you wouldn't stand for it, then don't do it.

DOGS CHASE CATS – DOGS CHASE CATS

DOGS OR NO DOGS

Guests are briefed on the rules regarding dogs; no dogs upstairs or on the furniture, all dogs must be dried before entering the property, no dogs must be left in the property alone, and at night, they must be in a cage. You can choose to relax this or stipulate more rules depending on your property's situation.

I have a posh cat, a beautiful ragdoll, so I often want to go away but don't want to leave my cat on her own, so I do welcome house cats. I suggest you also have a set of rules they sign before they bring their favourite furry friend. I am pretty strict. And don't be afraid to advise – they will have to leave if they don't follow the rules.

DOGS CHASE CATS

MEDIA COVERAGE

Is it Worth It?

The answer simply is yes; what may seem an arduous task of contacting the press every week may seem laborious and unnecessary, but yes, it pays off. At one point, I was in so many publications I got a bit blasé about it! If you are in a magazine, it gives kudos to your let. Think of a let as a product; you are selling a lifestyle retreat, a commodity to be taken seriously.

It would help if you went way further than the extra mile, and your recommendations and repeat bookings will flood in.

How to get into a publication:

It's reasonably simple to do all the hard work, write a blog and keep them updated or use Instagram to sell a story, use Pinterest and do a board on your product – your let. Mine would be called Turtledove Hideaway, and I would pin pictures from my website on my board which gets shared on the forum.

Someone may type in places to stay, country retreat, or chic holiday let, and if you have done your homework, yours will pop up, and they will pin it, which will take them straight to your website.

HAPPY CUSTOMERS – GREAT REVIEWS

PRESS ARTICLES

An Italian magazine, Casa da Sogno – January 2014

MEDIA – PUBLICITY – SUCCESS – REVIEWS

Wedding Magazine, November 2013 -
https://cdn.shopify.com/s/files/1/1723/5225/files/wedding-magazine-hits-turtledove.pdf?99595388829611753170

Evening Standard – Homes & Properties November 2013

The Telegraph – October 2013 – This Is Money

The Sunday Times (online) – October 2013

Wales online -
https://www.walesonline.co.uk/lifestyle/welsh-homes/rural-welsh-dream-home-could-14869849
Shropshire Star Newspaper -
https://cdn.shopify.com/s/files/1/1723/5225/files/The_Shropshire_B_B_._._._in_a_garage_Shropshire_Star.pdf?12305175077893179505

Westwing Magazine (Germany) – June 2013 -
http://www.westwing.de/magazin/inspirationen/cottage-living/
Home Bunch (Canada) – May 2013

Ideal Home magazine – July Issue 2014

Living North Magazine -
https://cdn.shopify.com/s/files/1/1723/5225/files/living-north-

MEDIA – GERMANY – CANADA

At the point of this book's first version going to press, Ideal Home magazine had contacted us and we would be in the July 2014 issue.

Ristrutturare Con Casa Chic – October 2013
https://cdn.shopify.com/s/files/1/1723/5225/files/wedding-magazine-hits-turtledove.pdf?99595388829611753170

MEDIA – PUBLICITY – SUCCESS – REVIEWS

House Beautiful – May 2013 – Renovation of the Year
https://cdn.shopify.com/s/files/1/1723/5225/files/house-
beautiful-may-2013-25.pdf?9906759780127643956

MEDIA – PUBLICITY – SUCCESS – REVIEWS

PRESS ARTICLES

Homebuilders and Renovators Magazine
https://cdn.shopify.com/s/files/1/1723/5225/files/homebuilders
-and-renovators-ma-29.pdf?17037618058509497798

MEDIA – PUBLICITY – SUCCESS – REVIEWS

TURTLEDOVE HIDEAWAY REVIEWS

"Tremendous, Attentive Host"

Thank you for a fantastic stay at Turtledove Hideaway! We have had a wonderful, cosy time at the cottage, which Kerrie decorated so beautifully for Christmas. Our highlights included: a delicious lunch and brilliant atmosphere at the Cross Foxes (dog friendly!); a day trip to Chester – great shopping, restaurant and history; a walk around Ellesmere Lake (good for wildlife spotting); and a knock at the door from Kerrie's daughter Jasmin bearing a delicious Christmas cake. Kerrie has been a tremendous and attentive host; all the best of luck for the future – we'll keep our eyes out for your brilliant work. Thanks again.

"Extra Mile"

I can't recommend this place highly enough, and we're hoping to come back again for sure. Kerrie, her partner and daughter Jasmin really went the extra mile to make us feel welcome and like one of the family. Oh, and not forgetting the cat! We don't want to go home; this place is truly unique and truly inspiring; Kerrie, you are truly talented!

AMAZING INTERIORS – PERFECT PLACE

"A Happy Hideaway"

We stayed in Kerrie's ABSOLUTELY DELIGHTFUL "Turtledove Hideaway," set on the grounds of Wood Farm House. The welcome we received was warm; the hideaway's interior, as beautiful as the setting, was tranquil. A lazy bank holiday weekend of lie-ins and exploring the local area (Llangollen Steam Railway, Powys Castle) and we were utterly relaxed. Kerrie is the perfect hostess, and we couldn't have asked for a dreamier weekend away.

"An Idyllic Honeymoon"

We came to the Turtledove Hideaway with high hopes for our honeymoon, and we can honestly say we were not disappointed! Upon arrival, we were greeted with a warm and friendly welcome, including a cake with wedding candles in it, baked by Kerrie's daughter Jasmin, which was just gorgeous.

AMAZING INTERIORS – PERFECT PLACE

"Amazing Interiors"

Thank you for a lovely stay! We've really enjoyed being nice and cosy with the log fire and stunning surroundings. Thank you for the advice on where to visit; we had a lovely day out. It's incredible what you've done with the barn; we might ask you for some advice on our new home! Thank you.

"Perfect"

We had a lovely stay here over our three nights. The cottage was perfect for everything we needed and an excellent base for exploring the area. Thanks, Kerrie, for all the little touches and for making us feel so welcome.

"A Happy Getaway"

Thank you so much for welcoming us to Turtledove. We had a fantastic stay over the weekend, and your recommendations were spot on! You are a real inspiration when it comes to your interior design – we may even call on you in the future! We loved our stay in the cottage and hope to return again – we will definitely be recommending it to others.

AMAZING INTERIORS – PERFECT PLACE

"Highly Recommended"

We've had a fantastic long weekend at Turtledove Hideaway. We had high expectations after seeing the pictures – we were not disappointed! Kerrie has done a fabulous job with the cottage; it is beautiful and so cosy that we are sad to leave. Kerrie was an attentive and thoughtful host; she gave us several great tips, of which our favourite was Horseshoe Pass, followed by a fantastic lunch at the Corn Hill at Llangollen. I can't recommend it highly enough! Thank you, Kerrie, it has been a brilliant retreat from London. We are already planning a return visit.

"Amazing Birthday Stay"

We have had an amazing birthday stay, and we're sorry to be going. The cottage is gorgeous, and the surroundings are very peaceful. Thank you to Kerrie and her partner for making us so welcome. We had a day trip to Llangollen, where we walked down to the River Dee. It was a beautiful little village where we ended up in the Corn Mill pub/restaurant and had a wonderful meal. A must if you go there!

AMAZING INTERIORS – PERFECT PLACE

"Hideaway Breakfast"

What a wonderful weekend! I'm sad to have to leave – we certainly could have done with another day to explore the area especially given the lovely long lie-ins followed by Hideaway breakfast!

"Great Recommendations"

We had a really delightful four days in the cottage with our six-month-old puppy Harry. We enjoyed the times we spent in the cottage as much as the times away from it. Thank you for your recommendations, which we are delighted to recommend now as well, especially: Llangollen – lovely walks and views; Colemere – fab circular walk around the lake with Harry; Shrewsbury – good for independent shops.
Eating out – The Cross Foxes at Erbistock, really excellent food, best meal of the holiday, in particular duck three ways, roasted pigeon breast, and bread and butter pudding – best I've ever had. We also enjoyed taking care of the hens and enjoying their wonderful fresh eggs. PS, my very tall fella even managed not to bang his head when in the bedroom!

AMAZING INTERIORS – PERFECT PLACE

"Ultimate Triumph in Homemaking"

Yours is the ultimate triumph in homemaking;
you have created a place, which emanates the promise of happiness that can never subside. We are so grateful that you have shared this special place with us; we have been bowled over by your kind hospitality and Jasmin's extraordinary baking skills. We both look forward to seeing you on Celebrity Bake Off!

"Perfect Romantic Retreat"

Perfect romantic retreat following our wedding! Beautifully decorated and such a lovely, peaceful location – just what we needed! We'd recommend Llangollen and neighbouring villages. Ellesmere Lake is also a good day out. Thank you.

"Favourite Holiday Ever"

After just one day at Turtledove Hideaway, my boyfriend said, "This is my favourite holiday ever" – and I couldn't agree more. Never have we come across such an exquisite cottage – it really is idyllic, and we honestly didn't want to leave! We'd recommend climbing Snowdon while you're here.

EXTRA MILE – HIGHLY RECOMMENDED

We also went to Cheshire Oaks and Colemere for a lovely, easy walk. The Boat is a great place to eat, as is The Pheasant, where we went after the Sandstone trail and candle making. We'll undoubtedly be coming back! Thanks for everything; you're wonderfully creative, accommodating and thoughtful. You should be hugely proud of what you've done here; we'll be recommending you and Turtledove Hideaway to all and sundry.

DREAMY WEEKEND – ROMANTIC RETREAT

BATHROOM FITTINGS – ALL DETAILS AND PRICES:

Lux Stone pebble tile 300 x 600mm

Rectified edge – pre-sealed porcelain – suitable for wall and floor, £35.97 per square metre (approximately 5.5 tiles per m2)

Baskets from £20 – The Interior Co.co.uk

Soap and hand cream – Molton Brown

Towels from Homesense DKNY

Driftwood mirror, large – £165 The Interior co.co.uk

MOLTON BROWN – FLUFFY TOWELS

KITCHEN FITTINGS – ALL DETAILS AND PRICES

Doors

Two 715 x 596 Doors, BA Bella Range: Cambridge

Colour: Matt Olive – £29.28 ea.

One 715 x 396 Door, BA Bella Range: Venice

Colour: Matt Olive – £20.89

Two 2540 x 150 lengths plinth

Colour: Matt Olive – £22.86 ea.

One metre self-adhesive vinyl 620w

Colour: Matt Olive – £15.97 per metre

One 715 x 296 x 296 Curved Door, BA Bella Range: Venice

Colour: Matt Olive – £139.81

One 150 x 250 x 250 Curved Plinth

Colour: Matt Olive – £37.26

LANTERNS – SAILING BOATS

All above from Kitchen Door Swap

Carcass and worktops from Vision Kitchen Design, Oxford

The worktop, from Vision Kitchen Designs in Oxford, is called Mistral

Worktop: The material can be fabricated and joined etc., in many ways so that the price can be primarily labour cost, but for this project, there was one length of approx. 3m and no special fabricating. This would be about £650 retail.

Sales: 0844 874 7299

Kitchen Door Swap supplied the doors, and Vision Kitchens supplied the worktops and carcasses.

Mini Biselado Metro Perla kitchen tiles 75 x 150mm

Suitable for wall only, £29.92 m2 (88 tiles per m2 approx. Colour Supplies Wrexham)

The toaster was a Magimix Two Slot, retailing at £120.00

from House makers www.housemakers.co.uk

Chapati board The Interior Co

Compost bucket £14 The Interior Co

Oars £39.99

Distressed wooden flower sign The Interior Co

CLOCKS – HEARTS – BOOKS

The mattress was Prince, retailing at £99.99 from Colour Supplies, Mount Street Retail Park, Wrexham, LL13 8DW.

The below came from www.housemakers.co.uk

The bed is a Highgrove, retailing at £391.20.

The bedside cabinets are also Highgrove retailing at £87.99.

Natural tab top curtain pair – £149 The Interior Co

Laurel leaf curtain header or bed header – £99 The Interior Co

Slate scallop edge quilt – £240 The Interior Co

Slate oversized scalloped edge cushion cover – £42.99 The Interior Co.

Forest scent dark grey heart – £8.99 The Interior Co

FRENCH WALL LIGHTS – SCENTED CANDLES

Wood lantern with rope handles – The Interior Co.
Wood lantern – w: 230mm h: 320mm – £99.99 The Interior Co
Henna heart – £12.99, £19.99, £29.99 The Interior Co

LIVING AREA FITTINGS – ALL DETAILS AND PRICES

Sofa refurbished 1920s drop arm sofa, in designers' guild – £899
Linen two-seater sofa – £899 The Interior Co
"Kensington" wall clock – £69 The Interior Co
Paperwhite plants in pot – £48.99 put in a small candle holder on wicker plate £12.99 The Interior Co.
"Beech/brass" tripod lamp – £225 The Interior Co
French wall lamp with grey linen shade – £48.99 The Interior Co
White orchid in square basket – £59.99 The Interior Co
Navy, cream bunting – £19.99 The Interior Co.
Wooden bird peg – £8.99 The Interior Co
Sandpipers – £32.99 The Interior Co
Deerskin rug – £165 The Interior Co
Bird nesting shack – £54.00 The Interior Co

FRENCH WALL LIGHTS – SCENTED CANDLES

SHOPPING

Brown leather-look shoe – £15.99 The Interior Co
Industrial nest of tables, zinc – £357 The Interior Co
Original canvas 05 – £395, Release painting feather
By Kerrie Griffin, available online from The Interior Co
Oak and iron console – £449 The Interior Co
Natural tab top curtain pair – £149 The Interior Co
 Limewash Deep framed mirror – £145 The Interior Co
Polo cushions – £34.99 The Interior Co
Polo napkins from £8 all The Interior Co
The curtain poles were a range called Lite FX – 3m, £24.98, 1.8m £17.99 and the 1.2m, £14.99 available in Brushed Chrome, Antique Brass & Black Nickel. From Colour Supplies, Mount Street Retail Park, Wrexham, LL13 8DW.
Pet bed – £72 The Interior Co
Memo board – £38 The Interior Co.
Cream sailboat – £99 The Interior Co

FRENCH WALL LIGHTS – SCENTED CANDLES

OFFICE/DINING FITTINGS - ALL DETAILS AND PRICES

Banbury Hall table – £429 The Interior Co

FRENCH WALL LIGHTS – SCENTED CANDLES

Pet bed – £72 The Interior Co
Memo board – £38 The Interior Co.
Cream sailboat – £99 The Interior Co

FRENCH WALL LIGHTS – SCENTED CANDLES

Accessories from The Interior Co

MIRRORS - CUSHIONS

Create a welcoming entrance

Windows and Doors - all details and prices
Windows £50 each.
The second-hand door used from the old utility room.
Solid Oak door from Morgans of Oswestry for the bathroom. It's worth asking if they have any seconds as I was cutting the corner off to fit into the cat-slide area at the back of the building as a bathroom door.

BAY TREES – SAILBOATS

I found one at Morgans, which was slightly damaged; in the top corner, they reduced it from £249 down to £80, the internal frame was £34. I shopped around, and Morgans came out at the best price.

Timber cladding - details and £65 ETC Chirk, Wrexham

Bathroom fittings - I bought the sink taps and shower from Victoria Plumb. It was the most stylish and the best price on the market, and do shop around.

The fixtures and sink were both £69. The shower screen was £199 with a free shower tray. I then bought the electric shower from Homebase, which was on offer for £89. I made the washstand legs from three-by-two leftover timber and used planks from a pallet for the shelves; the top is Mistral stone off-cut Free.

Wood Farm House Boutique Rooms

Country Bedroom Designed By Kerrie Griffin
Award Winning Interior Designer

BOUTIQUE-ACCOMMODATION

Wood Farm House Boutique Rooms

"Wood Farm House Bed & Breakfast is a great oak-framed house built around five hundred years ago, situated in stunning countryside on the borders of Cheshire, Shropshire and Wales. The owner, Artist and Interior Designer Kerrie Griffin-Rogers, has transformed Wood Farm House into the talking point of magazines Country Homes & Interiors, Ideal Homes and other leading publications. You'll feel a million miles from anywhere but are only 5 miles away from the award-winning wedding venue of Iscoyd Park. Bangor on Dee Racecourse is only a ten-minute drive, as is the must-visit for any birdwatcher – Ellesmere. National Trust properties Powys Castle, Erddig Hall and Chirk Castle, are a short drive away, as is the Roman City of Chester and historic Shrewsbury. Only a little further, and you can be among the biggest and boldest mountains in Wales or England – Snowdonia! The house is set in approximately 150 acres of rolling countryside, up a private road. The rooms are creatively lavished with items from her interior company and her art, which you can buy.

BOUTIQUE-ACCOMMODATION

They have beautiful beams, white bed linen, great accessories (all available to buy) and are painted in F&B Paint, a must with our owner. She sets a warm, friendly atmosphere, attracting guests yearning for a bit of history and indulgence in the world of interiors and art in a spacious and intimate guesthouse where everyone is treated like family. You have the fabulous old thirty-foot lounge all to yourself, beams everywhere, Wi-Fi and television (should you need!) for the duration of your stay, and a tranquil private garden area. Kerrie also has a boutique with her brand of affordable Italian clothing range – Feathers of Italy. She is featured in 25 Beautiful Homes magazine on page 126, September.

GREAT REVIEWS-INCOME

This little seat I made from offcuts of wood is
a great warm welcome when guests arrive.

COUNTRY-LIVING

Wood Farm House Boutique Rooms - Reviews

"Wood Farm House - Superb in Every Sense"

Reviewed 15 December 2013

It is probably best to use your sat nav to find Wood Farm House, although it is not too tricky with a map. However, the windy roads and country lanes are well worth navigating to reach this wonderful retreat. We were going to arrive late and texted Kerrie (the owner) to say so – "Gin and Tonic or a cup of tea?" was her reply! This sums up how well you are looked after and how welcome you are made to feel. We stayed for two nights for a wedding nearby, and Kerrie could not do enough for us. The house, rooms and cottage outside are rustic, stylish and of sheer quality. Coffee, tea on hand; continental breakfast or traditional cooked breakfast – we had both, and they too were excellent. We enjoyed an extra treat since Kerrie's lovely daughter Jasmine was home and helped her Mum with everything. The most crucial point to note is how peaceful the place is; you relax when you step across the threshold and wish you stayed longer when the time comes to leave. Cannot speak highly enough of this Wood Farm House – we travel a lot, and this rates with the very best, bar none.

Room Tip: Pick any of them

HAPPY CUSTOMERS

Wood Farm House Boutique Rooms - Reviews

"A Warm Welcome for All the Family"

Reviewed 24 September 2013

We stayed with Kerrie in the B&B for a wedding at nearby Iscoyd Park. We were two couples with three kids between us, my Mum who kindly babysat for us. The accommodation was very stylish and comfortable, and a real highlight for the children was collecting fresh eggs for the fabulous full English breakfast the following day! The setting is simply stunning, and we are so glad we had the opportunity to find this little gem that we wouldn't have come across without the wedding!

"Immaculate homely atmosphere, very relaxing surroundings and excellent hospitality from the whole family."

EXPAND-RECYCLE-UPCYCLE-B&B

Wood Farm House Boutique Rooms - Reviews

Wood Farm House with Turtledove Hideaway in the backdrop.

"Beautiful, Tranquil Spot"

After a few miles of winding lanes, you eventually arrive at a beautiful, tranquil spot, and behind the gates of Wood Farm House is a lovely home. Everything from the initial welcome and friendliness of the family was outstanding. The rooms are beautifully decorated with lots of personal touches, such as original artwork and accessories, which you can also purchase.

TRANQUIL-ORIGINAL ARTWORK

Wood Farm House Boutique Rooms - Reviews

We were given lots of advice on places to eat and were made to feel that their home was indeed ours for the duration of our stay. The breakfast was well cooked and served in a beautiful lounge that we had sole use during our stay. Their young daughter, who had baked us some delicious cupcakes for the evening, provided an extra personal touch. I would not hesitate to stay there again and recommend it to friends.

"Wonderful Retreat"

We stayed with Kerrie at the end of November and have been meaning to leave a review ever since. After a full day out in Liverpool, we drove over there and only wish we'd got there earlier. Beautiful house with a lovely ambience. Kerrie cooked a wonderful meal, and we took some champagne, which we drank in the lounge in front of the log fire. Left the next day after a great breakfast feeling thoroughly chilled – would happily return for longer or recommend to anyone.

GREAT BREAKFAST-THOROUGHLY CHILLED

Wood Farm House Boutique Rooms - Reviews

Guests were allowed to use this 32-foot lounge.

WONDERFUL RETREAT – WARM WELCOME

Wood Farm House Boutique Rooms - Reviews

"Thoroughly Recommended"

We had a great weekend here; the hostess is fantastic, made us feel very welcome. House is in a tranquil place, so you sleep really well. It's really tastefully done up as the owner is an artist and interior designer. Felt like a home from home, and we thoroughly recommend it.

DELICIOUS CUPCAKES – ORGANIC FOOD

Project 2 The Horse has a better view!

See this? It's a stable block now, but I feel the need to build Turtledove Hideaway No Two.

I keep going into the stables thinking the horses have impressive views; you may say it was wasted on the horses, but hopefully, you will see this next in a glossy monthly interiors' magazine, the national press, and finally for rent.

MULTI-AWARD-WINING ENTREPRENEUR SEEKS NEXT CHALLENGE

WHAT'S NEXT? PROJECT TWO

After that, I plan to extend the Farmhouse giving a 49 percent increase in space. I already have planning permission; I'm just on the lookout for an ingenious, cost-effective idea to do it. I would love to timber-clad it to make it look New England style.
Wish me luck.

Look out for my other books coming soon and my novel *Bullshit, and Half, a Dozen Eggs.*

You can contact me at
info@theinteriorco.co.uk www.theinteriorco.co.uk
07500 930207
https://www.turtledovehideaway.co.uk

DELICIOUS CUPCAKES – ORGANIC FOOD

STOP PRESS

As we were going to press in 2014, we had the great news that Theo Paphitis had chosen The Interior Co to promote on his website, http://www.theopaphitissbs.com, where we are now a lifetime member. Kerrie met Theo that November to collect her award.

The Interior Co
The Winner, Sunday, 3 March 2014

THEO PAPHITI S – ENTREPRENEUR

The initiative, Small Business Sunday, shortened to the hashtag #SBS on Twitter, was created by Theo Paphitis of Dragon's Den fame and was founded in October 2010. Every Sunday, small businesses can tweet Theo directly to describe their business to him in 140 characters or less. Theo then reviews the thousands of entries and chooses just six to re-tweet to his over 400,000 followers, which can mean a massive publicity boost and increased sales for the selected few lucky businesses.

Kerrie said, "I have been following the #SBS initiative for the last couple of years and have persevered to get the chance to be recognised. I couldn't believe it when my business was chosen on Sunday, 3 March. Theo gets over 1,500 tweets every week from small businesses, so I am absolutely delighted to have been selected and passed on to his many followers. We have received 1,633 tweets in 48 hours, as well as over 100 extra followers, and this is increasing all the time." Since writing this book in 2014 I have gone on to win a few more awards, making me a multi-award-winning interior designer. It took a lot of courage to start again and succeed after a divorce and fighting depression. In 2019, I felt it was the time to speak out about it and I won an award for courage.

MULTI – AWARD WINNING ENTREPRENEUR

Winner Sunday 3rd March 2014

Theo Helped me realise I was doing alright!

THEO PAPHITI S – KERRIE GRIFFIN

CONTACT

FEATHER PRESS

PUBLISHING

If you would like to learn more about my work, you can reach me at the email address below. I am in the process of starting a company selling you a turn-key Turtledove Hideaway for your very own garden. If you are interested in more details, then either sign up for my newsletter on my website or drop me a line, and I will keep you updated on my progress.

I hope you have enjoyed reading my story, and I hope lots of little bijou boltholes will appear after lockdown for some quirky places for us all to stay. Keep being creative. theinteriorco.co.uk

Kerrie Griffin
Multi-Award-Winning Interior Designer
info@theinteriorco.co.uk

THEO PAPHITI S – KERRIE GRIFFIN

CONTACT info@theinteriorco.co.uk

CONTACT Kerrie@theinteriorco.co.uk

THEO PAPHITI S – KERRIE GRIFFIN

CONTACT www.feathersofitaly.co.uk

CONTACT   www.turtledovehideaway.co.uk

THEO PAPHITI S – KERRIE GRIFFIN

2019/20/21 AWARDS

CorporateLiveWire

CENTRAL ENGLAND
PRESTIGE AWARDS

2020/21 WINNER

INTERIOR DESIGNER OF THE YEAR – CHESHIRE

CorporateLiveWire

MANCHESTER
& NORTH WEST
PRESTIGE AWARDS

2020/21 WINNER

INTERIOR DESIGN SPECIALIST OF THE YEAR –
Manchester & North West England Prestige Awards

KERRIE GRIFFIN

Winner of Positive Awards for Courage in adversity Nov 2019.

Featured in The Great Scottish Indoors Contemporary Scottish Styling website February 2021. Professional stylist and columnist Alison Gibs from Scotland

Cheshire Life 2021 March/April edition 6 page focus on my work.

CHESHIRE LIFE – POSITIVITY AWARDS

Talacre Beach, North Wales Taken by Kerrie Griffin

Printed in Great Britain
by Amazon

81065971R00083